AF290306

VINCENT VAN GOGH

A tortured genius

Written by Eliane Reynold de Seresin
In collaboration with Anthony Spiegeler
Translated by Emma Hanna

VINCENT VAN GOGH

- **Born:** 30 March 1853 in Zundert (Netherlands).
- **Died:** 29 July 1890 in Auvers-sur-Oise (France).
- **Context:** Postimpressionism.
- **Notable works:**
  - *The Potato Eaters* (1885), painting
  - *A Pair of Shoes* (1886), painting
  - *The Sunflowers* (1888), painting
  - *The Sower* (1888), painting
  - *The Starry Night* (1889), painting
  - *Bedroom in Arles* (1889), painting
  - *Self-Portrait with Bandaged Ear* (1889), painting

Vincent van Gogh was a Dutch painter who was greatly influenced by the social upheaval that characterised the 19th century. He was a religious individual who struggled with depression and the challenges of pursuing an unconventional career, and drew inspiration from the work of French realist authors, Dutch painters and the pastoral works of French artist Jean-François Millet (1814-1875) for inspiration. Today, he is remembered both for the genius of his work and for his struggles with his mental health.

Van Gogh found inspiration in both the Impressionist movement and Japonism, but went on to develop a distinctive artistic style that set him apart from other artists who were active at that time. Painting also provided him with an outlet as his mental health deteriorated. In Van Gogh's work, the subject of the painting is rarely just a simple object: in most cases, it also acts as a reflection of the artist's subconscious mind. Furthermore, the vibrant colours, frenetic execution and curved lines of Van Gogh's work paved the way for the rise of two other significant art movements: Fauvism and Expressionism. Although Van Gogh was deeply misunderstood during his lifetime and died in obscurity, his work was nothing less than revolutionary, and truly shaped 20th-century art.

CONTEXT

THE CALM AFTER THE STORM

After a number of uprisings and revolutions earlier in the 19th century, France entered a period of relative economic stability under the Second Empire (1852-1870). Industry was booming and new methods of communication were appearing, along with modern innovations such as railways, banks and department stores. This coincided with the rise of the middle class, and the job market was revitalised by strong economic growth. Furthermore, the 1860s were a period of political liberalisation, as Emperor Napoleon III (1808-1873) granted the right to strike in 1864 as a means of boosting his popularity, and granted parliament the right to interpellation four years later.

However, this era of peace and prosperity descended into turmoil when Napoleon III followed in the footsteps of his uncle Napoleon I (French Emperor, 1769-1821) by declaring war on Prussia on 19 July 1870. He was quickly defeated at the

Battle of Sedan less than two months later, leading to the establishment of the Third French Republic (1870-1940), but Paris was nevertheless besieged by Prussian forces for several months. This led to the Paris Commune, an unprecedented political uprising in March 1871 which saw the proletariat challenge the authority of the Third Republic. The Commune was founded on the tenets of socialism, which had emerged in 1820, and demanded a better quality of life for France's working-class citizens, as a lack of meaningful social progress meant that the country's newfound economic prosperity in the previous decades had not brought the same benefits for them as it had for the upper classes. However, the Third Republic soon regained control, and the establishment of the French Constitutional Laws of 1875 finally restored political stability. Van Gogh travelled to France for the first time that year.

MODERN LIFE VS. RURAL LIFE

Advances in metallurgy led to the invention of lighter, more malleable construction materials. This in turn led to a large-scale renovation of Paris (1853-1870) led by Baron Haussmann (French architect, 1809-1891), in accordance with Napoleon III's goal of transforming Paris into "the capital of capitals".

Thanks to the development of the railway network, it became possible to travel quickly and easily between Paris and the surrounding countryside, much to the delight of the city's inhabitants, who were now able to discover the joys of a day spent on the banks of the River Seine at their leisure. However, the citizens of rural France, who tended to be more conservative, were much less thrilled by both this sudden influx of city-dwellers and the advent of machinery, whereas supporters of the Republic embraced these changes and the modern ideals they were based on. As society inexorably moved into the modern era, the frenzied rate of progress created a certain degree of social hysteria which left many individuals troubled. Many artists denounced the problems caused by modern life and idealised the benefits of rural life, which they believed was intrinsically better for humanity. Van Gogh, who was among their number, frequently emphasised the simplicity of country life and the beauty of nature in his paintings, for example in *The Sower* (1888).

THE RISE OF REALISM

Although a certain degree of idealism flourished in culture under the Second Empire, the dawn of the modern era resulted in rising interest in artistic realism. For example, the French writers Gustave Flaubert (1821-1880), Guy de Maupassant (1850-1893) and Émile Zola (1840-1902) carefully crafted accurate, faithful reflections of everyday life in their works, thus offering readers a new perspective on society – which, incidentally, had a significant influence on Van Gogh. Meanwhile, the French painters Jean-François Millet and Gustave Courbet (1819-1877) acted as the figureheads of two different art movements that emerged in the mid-19th century, namely the Barbizon school and realism. Painters from the Barbizon school drew inspiration from both the Dutch masters and English landscape artists, and took nature and everyday life as their preferred subjects, as they identified more with these scenes than the historical subjects favoured by the Académie des Beaux-Arts.

Jean-François Millet moved to the French village of Barbizon in 1849, and during his time there he helped to found the Barbizon school, an art movement which sought to celebrate rural life. Nature was the main subject of their paintings, and they generally painted outside, a technique which was also used by the Impressionists in later years. Aside from Millet, the most influential members of the Barbizon school were the French painters Jean-Baptiste Camille Corot (1796-1875), Narcisse Díaz de la Peña (1807-1876), Théodore Rousseau (1812-1867) and Charles-François Daubigny (1817-1878).

These artists benefitted from scientific progress, notably the invention of paint tubes by John Goffe Rand (American artist, 1801-1873) in 1841, which enabled them to paint outside, and the invention of photography in 1826 by Joseph Nicéphore Niépce (French inventor, 1765-1833), which made it possible to capture the image of a moment in time. Their works tended to idealise rural life, presenting it as a paradise that was uncorrupted by the evils of modern society and rampant industrialisation. This meant that many of the painters from the Barbizon school withdrew to the countryside, as its tranquillity was much more to their liking than the hustle and bustle of the city.

Van Gogh was strongly influenced by both the Dutch masters and Millet's work; for example, some of his works bear strong similarities to Millet's paintings *The Sower* (1850) and *Noonday Rest* (1866). Millet's style also influenced the Impressionist movement, which was another major source of inspiration for Van Gogh.

THE INFLUENCE OF IMPRESSIONISM

Impressionism was an artistic movement led by the nonconformist French painter Édouard Manet (1832-1883) which rejected the strict rules of the French art world. At this time, art was becoming homogenous: sketches, historical subjects, universality and references to classical mythology had become predominant at the expense of all other subject matter. However, the Impressionists pushed back against these trends by emphasising the subjectivity of their own perspectives, choosing to paint landscapes or aspects of daily life and using bright colours, which were dabbed onto the canvas in small, fragmented quantities to evoke the shifting, ephemeral quality of natural light. The movement's first major exhibition was held in 1874, a year before Van Gogh's first visit to France.

The Impressionists were always on the lookout for potential new subjects for their paintings, and found inspiration in Japanese art, which began trickling into Europe after the isolationist policy of *Sakoku* was lifted in the mid-19th century. Indeed, the pavilion dedicated to Japanese art at the International Exposition of 1867 in Paris caused a sensation, as many young artists such as Edgar Degas (French painter, 1834-1917) and Claude Monet (French painter, 1840-1926) were drawn to these unfamiliar art forms, which included the printing technique *ukiyo-e* (literally "pictures of the floating world"). Van Gogh's intuitive understanding of art styles meant that he quickly grasped the potential represented by these Japanese prints, and he was able to incorporate their fluid brushstrokes, use of perspective, black outlines, distinctive layouts and emphasis on nature into his own work.

Japan maintained an isolationist policy known as *Sakoku* (which literally means "closed country") for more than two centuries, between 1641 and 1853. However, it ended when the Convention of Kanagawa was signed on 31 March 1854 following an expedition led by the American Commodore Matthew Perry (1794-1858). From this point onwards, Japan began trading with the rest of the world again.

BIOGRAPHY

A FAMILY OF ARTISTS AND PREACHERS

Vincent van Gogh was born in Zundert in the Netherlands on 30 March 1853. He was born a year to the day after an older brother who had died in infancy, and was given his dead brother's name. He was the oldest of six children, with the exception of his deceased elder brother, and his father was a preacher. Although relatively little is known about his relationships with most of the rest of his family, we do know that he was very close to his youngest brother Theodorus, nicknamed Theo (Dutch art dealer, 1857-1891), as they maintained correspondence throughout their lives and over 600 of the letters they exchanged have been preserved. Theo provided his brother with unfailing financial and emotional support throughout his entire life.

It was traditional for the members of the Van Gogh family to become either preachers or art dealers, and the young Vincent was no exception: in 1869, he began working in an art gallery in The Hague called Goupil & Cie, which was managed by one of his uncles. This large city seemed to suit the young artist's temperament better than his hometown, as he was able to spend his time visiting museums and discovering the work of the Dutch masters, and was quick to grasp the principles of art dealing. Over the next few years he worked in a number of the gallery's different branches, including those in London, Brussels and finally Paris, where he moved in 1875. However, he was eventually fired as a result of his reluctance to treat the art the dealership sold as mere merchandise.

At this time he was also rejected by a woman he had fallen in love with, and sought solace in religion. In 1876, he spent some time working as an assistant to a Methodist minister in London, and in 1878 he sat the entrance exam for the theology course offered by the University of Amsterdam, which he failed. Nevertheless, he decided to travel to the mining region of Borinage near Mons in Belgium, where he began working as an evangelist. His empathy drove him to live in the same squalid conditions as the people he was preaching to, but the intensity of his enthusiasm proved intimidating for those around him.

In 1880, he enrolled in the Académie Royale des Beaux-Arts of Belgium, where he met the Dutch painter Anthon van Rappard (1858-1892), with whom he developed a close friendship. However, in 1881 he spent some time in Etten, where his parents were now living, and his time with them sparked a great deal of conflict: his father even attempted to have him committed to an asylum, as his mental health was already showing signs of deteriorating before he turned 30. However, this was also when he discovered his calling as an artist.

SEEKING SOLACE IN PAINTING

Van Gogh returned to The Hague, where he devoted himself to painting and met his second cousin, Anton Mauve (1838-1888), who was a successful painter and taught Van Gogh a number of painting techniques, including perspective and the use of watercolour. Van Gogh also familiarised himself with the work of the Dutch and Flemish masters such as Peter Paul Rubens (1577-1640), Frans Hals the Elder (c. 1582-1666) and Rembrandt (1606-1669), and began reading the works of realist authors such as Honoré de Balzac (French writer, 1799-1850) and Charles Dickens (British writer, 1812-1870). In 1881, he met Sien Hoornik (1850-1904), a prostitute who already had one child and was pregnant with a second, but his family dissuaded him from pursuing a relationship with her.

After a brief stay in Drenthe, Van Gogh moved to Neunen in the southern Netherlands for two years, from 1883 to 1885. During his time there, he courted a woman named Margot Begemann, but his family opposed this match as well, which led Begemann to attempt suicide.

During this time, Van Gogh painted many rural scenes in dark tones reminiscent of the work of Rembrandt. This was also when he painted his first masterpiece, *The Potato Eaters* (1885), after sketching around 30 studies for it. His father died of a heart attack in March 1885, after which he travelled to Antwerp to study Fine Art. It was during his time there that he discovered Japanese prints.

In 1886 he decided to return to Paris, where his brother Theo was working as the director of the local branch of the Goupil gallery. Through him, Van Gogh met a number of Impressionist painters, including Claude Monet, Camille Pissarro (Danish-French artist, 1830-1903), Paul Gauguin (French artist, 1848-1903), Georges Seurat (French artist, 1859-1891) and Henri de Toulouse-Lautrec (French artist, 1864-1901), whose influence led him to start using brighter colours in his own work. He also became friends with the paint grinder and art dealer Julien Tanguy (1825-1894), nicknamed "Père Tanguy" ("Father Tanguy"), who traded with many of the popular artists of the era. Père Tanguy was the first person to exhibit Van Gogh's artwork, and Van Gogh painted his portrait on a number of occasions as a sign of gratitude.

However, living in the bustling French capital proved overwhelming for the anxious painter, and he eventually moved to the south of France to fully devote himself to his craft.

PAINTING THE SUNLIGHT

Van Gogh's arrival in the south of France coincided with a snowstorm, as though Provence was determined to welcome this northerner with a taste of his homeland. However, when the skies cleared, Van Gogh found himself deeply moved by the quality of light and the colours of the Mediterranean, which began featuring more and more prominently in his paintings. He became particularly fond of the colour yellow, as can be seen in his paintings *The Sunflowers* (1888), *Café Terrace at Night* (1888), *The Night Café* (1888) and *The Starry Night* (1889).

Van Gogh lived in relative isolation in Arles, as shown by the six self-portraits he painted during his time there (having previously painted around 20 others), but he dreamed of founding a community of artists. Paul Gauguin eventually joined him at the Yellow House, which was immortalised in several of Van Gogh's paintings, including *Bedroom in Arles* (1889). Although their collaboration started off well, tensions quickly arose and their time as housemates came to a dramatic end when Van Gogh cut his own ear off, as depicted in *Self Portrait with Bandaged Ear* (1889). This led the inhabitants of Arles to demand that the mayor banish Van Gogh or even commit him to an asylum.

Shortly afterwards, Van Gogh had another breakdown and was voluntarily admitted to the Saint-Paul asylum in Saint-Rémy-de-Provence. His brother Theo was worried by this situation, and implored him to move closer to him. As a result, Van Gogh moved to Auvers-sur-Oise on the northern outskirts of Paris in 1890, where he met Dr Paul Gachet (French physician, 1828-1909). Gachet was an admirer of modern art and a friend of the French painters Édouard Manet, Edgar Degas, Paul Cézanne (1839-1906) and Pierre-Auguste Renoir (1841-1919), and he quickly spotted Van Gogh's talent and acquired a number of his paintings. This was the beginning of an extremely prolific period of the artist's life, during which he painted approximately 70 paintings, including *The Church at Auvers* (1890), in just two months. However, on 27 July 1890, Van Gogh attempted to commit suicide while painting, and he died in his brother's arms two days later.

AN ILLUSTRIOUS LEGACY

With the exception of a handful of friends and relatives, the world did not mourn when Van Gogh died. Although his work had started to garner a measure of recognition in the final months of his life – indeed, the French art critic Gabriel-Albert Aurier (1865-1892) wrote an article for the literary review *Mercure de France* in 1890 in which he hailed Van Gogh as one of the leading figures of the avant-garde art scene – it all came too late for the Dutch artist, who only managed to sell a single painting (*The Red Vineyards near Arles*, 1888) during his lifetime. He bequeathed everything he owned to his brother Theo, meaning that Theo's wife Johanna van Gogh-Bonger (1862-1925) inherited almost the entirety of Van Gogh's artistic oeuvre when her husband died less than a year after his brother. She decided to ensure that her late brother-in-law's talent would not be forgotten, and published the complete correspondence between the two Van Gogh brothers in 1914. She also had Theo's body exhumed from his grave in Utrecht so that he could be reburied by his brother's side in the graveyard in Auvers-sur-Oise.

Although the first exhibitions of Van Gogh's work were organised by Julien Leclercq (French poet, 1865-1901) and Paul Cassirer (German art dealer, 1871-1926) in 1901, the exhibition held in the Stedelijk Museum in Amsterdam in 1905, which was financed by Van Gogh-Bonger, was particularly successful and marked a true turning point in the spread of Van Gogh's fame. Van Gogh-Bonger and Cassirer then began working together to organise future exhibitions; Van Gogh's work was exhibited in the United States for the first time just before the outbreak of the First World War (1914-1918). Finally, an exhibition of his work at the Museum of Modern Art in New York in 1930 brought his work to worldwide attention, and Van Gogh is now considered one of the greatest artists of the 19th century.

CHARACTERISTICS OF VAN GOGH'S WORK

A NATURALIST STYLE

Although Van Gogh's favoured artistic themes changed over the years, there can be no doubt that he was always particularly attuned to the hardships of other people. As the son of a preacher who struggled with depression throughout his life and often voluntarily lived in poverty, it is perhaps unsurprising that he was drawn to the masterpieces painted by the Flemish masters, which often featured normal people and scenes from daily life. Some notable examples of these works include the individual and group portraits produced by Frans Hals, such as *Meagre Company* (1633-1637), or *The Supper at Emmaus* (1629) and *The Night Watch* (1642) by Rembrandt. Many of Van Gogh's early works feature a similar use of dark tones and *chiaroscuro* (interplay of light and shadow).

Given Van Gogh's fondness for realist novels that also depicted the lives of the impoverished, it seems only fitting that in 1885, the same year that he finished *The Potato Eaters*, Émile Zola published his seminal work *Germinal*, which focused on the social justice movements which were growing in strength and popularity towards the end of the 19th century. Of course, Van Gogh also produced many other sketches and portraits of peasants, and he drew a great deal of inspiration from the work of the painter Jean-François Millet, particularly his preference for painting outdoors. Indeed, Millet's influence can be seen in a number of Van Gogh's paintings, especially those which depict farm work and the simple, hard-working lives of the peasantry such as *The Sower* (1888) and *The Siesta* (1889-1890). It seems clear that throughout his life, Van Gogh was simply searching for a source of simple happiness.

THE INFLUENCE OF THE "FLOATING WORLD"

Having discovered Japonism during his time in Antwerp, Van Gogh returned to Paris to find that the *ukiyo-e* ("pictures of the floating world") style had also become tremendously popular there in his absence. Many writers, journalists and business magnates, including Edmond de Goncourt (French art critic, 1822-1896), were fascinated by this "floating world" that was so different to Western art, and had begun collecting prints. Like many other painters of the era, Van Gogh began incorporating aspects of this style into his own work, including simple line-work, fluid brushstrokes, flat colours, a greater focus on nature and a lack of direct proportion between the frame and subject of the painting. Some of his works are even direct homages to Japanese prints, such as *Bridge in the Rain* (1887), which is a copy of *Sudden Shower over Shin-Ōhashi bridge and Atake* (1857) by Utagawa Hiroshige (Japanese artist, 1797-1858), and even the paintings which are considered most characteristic of Van Gogh's personal style feature hints of the influence of Japanese masters, such as *Olive Orchard* (1889).

It seems entirely probable that Van Gogh found the calm, harmony and order that characterises this Japanese style to be a source of comfort, even though it diverges significantly from his own style. Indeed, a joint exhibition of Van Gogh and Hiroshige's work was held in Paris from 2012 to 2013 in order to showcase the similarities and contrasts between their styles.

BURSTS OF COLOUR

Impressionism was another major source of inspiration for Van Gogh. His brother Theo featured a number of works by Impressionist artists in the gallery he managed in Paris, which enabled him to introduce his older brother to this revolutionary artistic movement when Vincent moved to Paris. The influence of the Impressionists led Van Gogh to focus more on painting outdoors, depicting nature as he saw it and using brighter colours in his work.

The work of the Impressionists generally explored light, colour and the fleeting nature of a moment in time, and Van Gogh's work soon began echoing these characteristics. He began using a greater variety of colours, which was made possible by the scientific advances which had allowed new pigments to be produced. He also drew on the law of complementary colours developed by Michel-Eugène Chevreul

(French chemist, 1786-1889) in 1839, and colour gradually became one of the driving forces in his work. More precisely, the colour yellow – one of the most vibrant, intense colours in the entire spectrum – eventually became one of the most characteristic features of his painting style.

CAPTURING THE SPIRIT OF THE ARTIST

The most distinctive aspect of Van Gogh's style is his tendency to depict curved lines, which is often interpreted as an unconscious reflection of his troubled mental state. Similarly, he often uses dark stripes reminiscent of the black rings of *ukiyo-e*, which add dynamism and a sense of movement to his work. Each of his paintings is carefully structured so that these lines seem to emanate from the main subject, thus emphasising its importance. This technique went against the artistic conventions of the time, which stipulated that the structure of a painting should be determined by external factors such as perspective, and that it should depict the real world in an objective manner, whereas the structure of Van Gogh's paintings was determined by their subjects, allowing the work as a whole to reflect the painter's state of mind. While the Impressionists had already rebelled against these artistic conventions, Van Gogh was the first artist to make his own psyche a part of his art. This made him a true pioneer, as these two concepts have become practically inseparable today: a painting is now generally considered an extension and reflection of the artist's own personality. Indeed, art is no longer intended to be the vehicle for a simple message, but a manifesto of the painter's personal philosophy.

The thick, staccato brushstrokes that characterise Van Gogh's work attest to the speed and ferocious energy with which he worked. The distorted lines that appear throughout his work seem to suggest that everything is in perpetual motion, and nothing is fixed or stable, which may be a reflection of the mental turmoil and pain he struggled with. In any case, this innovative means of expression revolutionised the very nature of art, and opened up new possibilities for generations of artists to come.

NOTABLE WORKS

THE POTATO EATERS

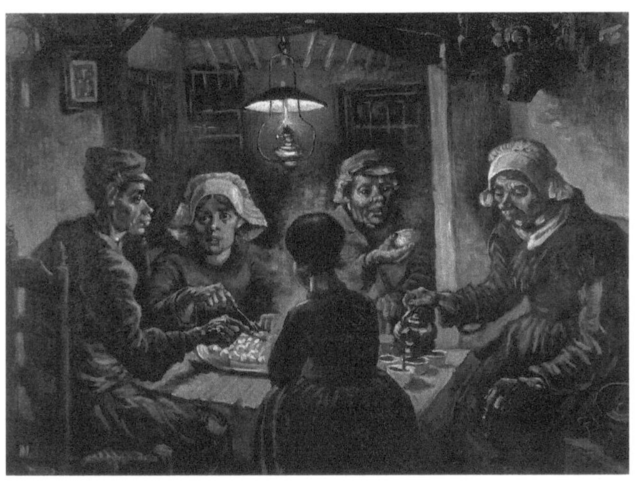

| *The Potato Eaters*, 1885, oil on canvas, 82 x 114 cm, Amsterdam, Van Gogh Museum.

The Potato Eaters is a celebration of peasantry and simplicity, and is considered Van Gogh's first masterpiece. It was painted while he was living in Neunen in 1885, and reflects his admiration for the Dutch masters. The use of dark colours echoes the peasants' rural way of life, and their gnarled hands attest to the hard work they carry out each day. Van Gogh praised the honesty and worthiness of the peasantry in one of his letters to his brother Theo: "and so [the painting] speaks of manual labour and — that they have thus honestly earned their food" (vangoghletters.org: 497).

The subjects' faces bear a certain similarity to their food, as they are unwashed, rugged and unique. The poorly-lit room highlights the isolation and poverty they live in, and the use of *chiaroscuro* is reminiscent of the works of Rembrandt. However, the light in the painting seems to emanate from the table instead of the lamp, which emphasises the role it plays as a meeting point and source of connection for the peasants and seems to suggest that the act of sharing has given them a source of true wealth. As the son of a preacher, it is perhaps unsurprising that Van Gogh was drawn to and moved by this Biblical conception of poverty.

Although the painting features the rapidly-executed brushstrokes typical of Van Gogh's work, he actually made over 30 studies before producing the final version. This masterpiece is one of the few paintings that Van Gogh was truly proud of for the rest of his life, and constitutes an important homage to Dutch painters, particularly Rembrandt, as well as providing us with key insight into the early development of Van Gogh's artistic style.

THE SOWER

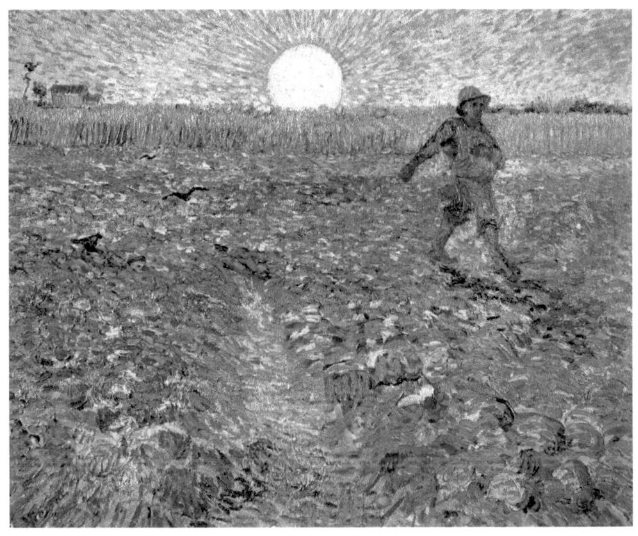

| *The Sower*, 1888, oil on canvas, 64 x 84.5 cm, Otterlo, Rijksmuseum Kröller-Müller.

The Sower is a direct homage to Millet's 1850 painting of the same name: not only do the paintings share a title, but Van Gogh also reproduces the same composition and positions his subject in the same way, although the execution is more modern in style; indeed, it is immediately obvious that the painting is typical of the Impressionist style. This is unsurprising, as it was produced just after Van Gogh's second sojourn in Paris, where he took an interest in divisionism and met several of the leading figures of Impressionism. As a result, he adopted a number of their techniques, including painting in the open air and colour juxtaposition. In this particular painting, the halo around the sun is reminiscent of pointillism, a technique that was popularised by Georges Seurat, of whom Van Gogh was an admirer.

Furthermore, it is no coincidence that the sower is a recurring theme in Van Gogh's work: it may even be a covert reference to the Biblical parable of the sower, which he undoubtedly listened to many times as a child. The theme of death is also omnipresent in this painting: the orange-tinted sun hangs low in the sky, signalling the end of the day, and the ears of wheat in the foreground have been cut down. However, it is worth noting that the painting exudes a peaceful atmosphere, which reflects Van Gogh's own attitude towards death at the moment he painted it. Indeed, while working on another painting called *The Reaper* (1889), Van Gogh said "I then saw the image of death in it, in this sense that humanity would be the wheat being reaped. So if you like it's the opposite of that Sower I tried before. But in this death nothing sad, it takes place in broad daylight with a sun that floods everything with a light of fine gold" (vangoghletters.org: 800).

POINTILLISM AND DIVISIONISM

Pointillism is a technique associated with Impressionism, specifically with its inventor Georges Seurat, and involves using small, distinct dots of colour to create a painting. Similarly, divisionism is a Postimpressionist technique which is based on the juxtaposition of two complementary colours, and is primarily associated with the work of Paul Signac (French painter, 1863-1935). While these two techniques are very similar, pointillism is solely concerned with the form of the brushstrokes, while divisionism also depends on the specific colours used. Given that both of these techniques emerged in the wake of Impressionism, they can more properly be said to belong to the Neo-Impressionist movement.

THE SUNFLOWERS

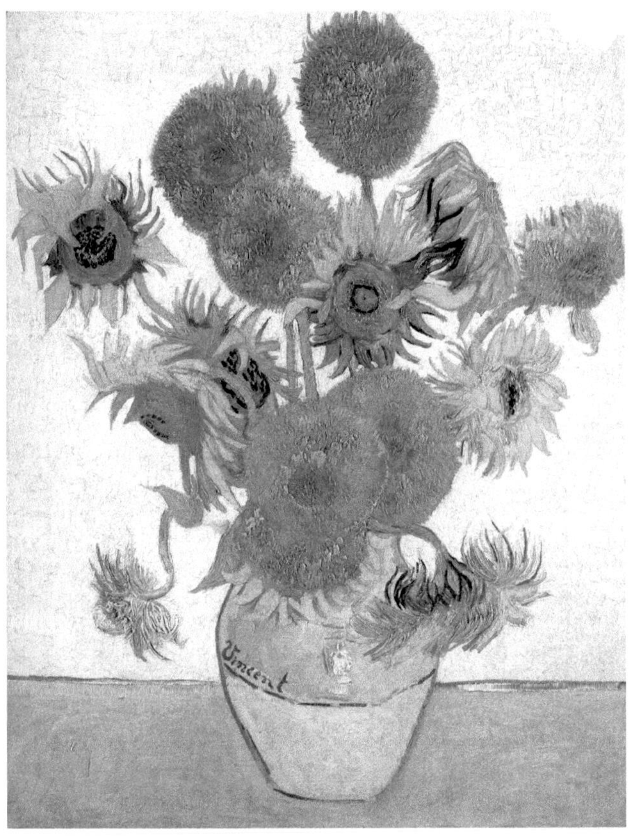

| *The Sunflowers*, 1888, oil on canvas, 92.1 x 73 cm,
London, National Gallery.

While Van Gogh began painting sunflowers during his time in Paris, it was not until he moved to Arles that this theme took on a life of its own. This is perhaps unsurprising, given that Arles is much sunnier than Paris, and Van Gogh's home there was literally known as "The Yellow House"!

His decision to paint the sunflowers was motivated by the impending arrival of his friend Paul Gauguin, which was supposed to be the first step towards Van Gogh's dream of creating a thriving community of artists. Wanting to decorate Gauguin's bedroom, he chose the theme of sunflowers as a way of expressing his admiration for the other painter.

Sunflowers became one of Van Gogh's fixations, and he went on to paint no fewer than seven versions of more or less the same still life over the course of his career. Of course, this reflects his fascination with sunlight, even though he also suffered from fevers as a result of the heat, which exacerbated his problems with his mental health.

Shades of yellow are predominant in this painting – and not just in the flowers themselves, but also in the vase, table and background. Indeed, it seems as though the flourishes of green, blue and brown merely serve to accentuate the overall impression of overwhelming yellow.

Monet had produced a similar still life of sunflowers in a vase seven years previously, and while Van Gogh had probably never seen this painting, Gauguin would certainly have been familiar with it. However, the styles used by the two painters are fundamentally different: while Monet's work is light and balanced, Van Gogh's painting is attention-grabbing and dynamic, with flowers that seem almost alive, thanks in particular to the thick brushstrokes. Furthermore, a closer look reveals that some of the flowers are still budding, while others are in full bloom and still others are already starting to wilt. The open sunflowers in their prime represent Van Gogh's full potential, while the wilting flowers represent his decline and the inner turmoil he was experiencing. In this way, the artist used the painting to express his innermost feelings, creating a veritable eulogy to life and death. Finally, while the colour yellow was one of the defining characteristics of Van Gogh's work throughout his entire career, especially during his time in Arles, it is never more in evidence than in this series of paintings.

THE STARRY NIGHT

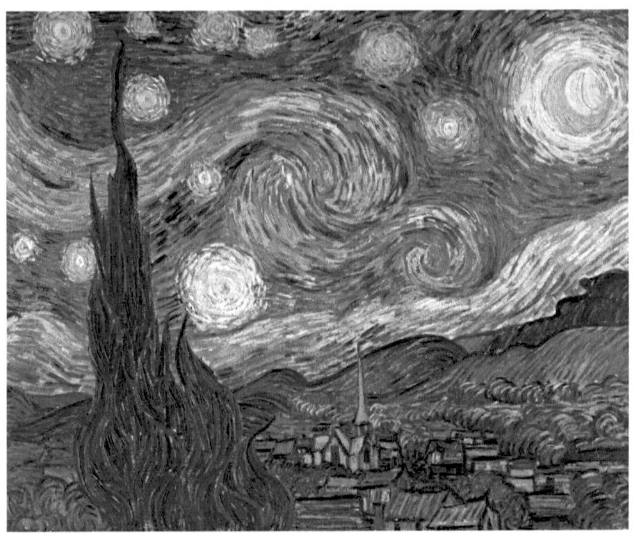

| *The Starry Night*, 1889, oil on canvas, 73.3 x 92.1 cm, New York, Museum of Modern Art.

Following a lengthy struggle with depression and several mental breakdowns, Van Gogh realised that he was no longer fit to live alone and was voluntarily admitted to the Saint-Paul asylum, which was housed in a former monastery. The institution provided him with a second room that he was able to use as an art studio, enabling him to continue painting incessantly, which was his only outlet.

Drawing inspiration from the colourful works of the Impressionists and from divisionism, Van Gogh chose to combine two primary colours (the yellow he frequently worked with in Arles and a shade of blue that represented Saint-Rémy-de-Provence, the town where the asylum was located) to create a powerful overall impression in this painting. The bright, radiant, feverish yellow tones are drowned in the calm blue of the sky, creating a sense of balance.

Although *The Starry Night* was produced in Van Gogh's bedroom, it is not a faithful depiction of the view from his window. Indeed, Van Gogh was unconcerned with accuracy, and instead simply used the landscape as a canvas for his own imagination. This painting is imbued with the full power of his creative energy, meaning that the end result is far more unique than a mere view of the countryside.

The cypress tree is one of the elements of the painting that was plucked from Van Gogh's imagination. It stretches far higher than it should, acting as a bridge between the earth and the sky, and is contorted in such a way that it resembles a menacing black flame licking skywards, almost like a signpost that directs us towards the spectacular sight lighting up the heavens. The shimmering stars seem to dance above the sleepy village, and rather than enclosing everything in restrictive boundaries, the swirling lines surrounding them, which are reminiscent of *ukiyo-e* prints, create the impression that the entire painting is moving in a feverish spiral pattern. The radiant starlight completely outshines the lights of the town, making it seem as though the modernity it represents is being dwarfed by the glory of nature.

The Starry Night was completed approximately eight months after *Starry Night Over the Rhône* (1888) and one year before the artist's death. While it certainly gives the viewer some insight into the mental turmoil he was experiencing, it also creates a vision of the glory of nature and transforms Van Gogh's drunken view into a breathtaking reminder of the immensity of space.

BEDROOM IN ARLES

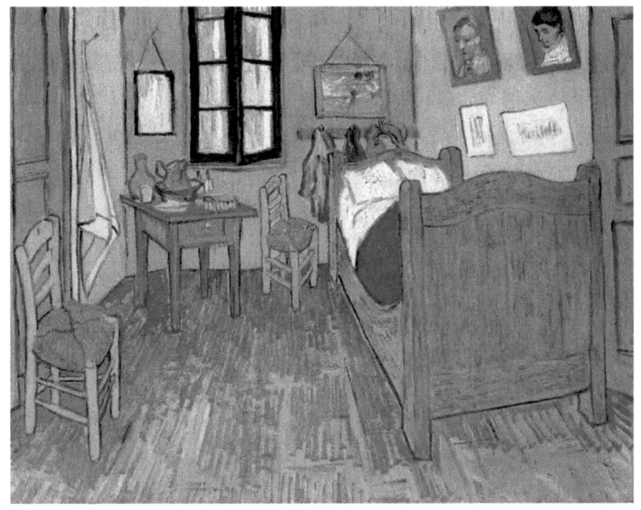

| *Bedroom in Arles*, 1889, oil on canvas, 57.3 x 73.5 cm, Paris, Musée d'Orsay.

Van Gogh painted several versions of his bedroom in Arles, of which this is the third. It is relatively similar to the two previous versions, although the original painting was damaged due to flooding during the artist's time in the asylum. In this painting, Van Gogh attempted to convey the extreme simplicity and monastic asceticism that defined his life, and even seems to compare it to the simplicity of Japanese bedrooms, despite the significant differences between them.

Although both of the portraits on the walls were of other painters in the previous versions, including the Belgian painter Eugène Boch (1855-1941), the painting on the left has been changed to a self-portrait in this painting. This is possibly because this new version was intended to be a present for his sister, or it could be a tribute to the works of the Flemish masters, which tended to include a nod to the owner of a property. The first version of this painting was completed just before Gauguin's visit, and the two empty chairs symbolise the fact that Van Gogh was waiting for him, while the closed window represents the seclusion he hoped they would share. The artist also plays with the painting's convergence lines, demonstrating his knowledge of the conventions that governed Renaissance art. This also introduces a certain lopsided instability to the painting's composition, which contrasts with the balance embodied by its content: almost every object in this room has a counterpart, which creates a sense of symmetry. The motif of pairs – which even includes two pillows – conveys the idea of couples and, by extension, stability, and could be Van Gogh's way of expressing the idea that he found some respite during his seclusion there.

Aside from the paintings hanging on the wall (which could, in theory, be merely decorative), there is nothing in the painting that makes it clear that this room belongs to an artist; there is not even a stray paintbrush acting as a clue. The only other hint comes in the form of the aprons hanging behind the bed, although they are barely visible. As such, this bedroom is presented as a kind of sanctuary where Van Gogh can rest and let go of the creative frenzy that acted as both a much-needed outlet and source of exhaustion for him. Blue is the predominant colour in this final version of the painting, and acts as a symbol of peace and calm, as he explained in a letter to Gauguin: "I had wished to express *utter repose* with all these very different tones" (vangoghletters.org: 706). However, we will never truly know what motivated Van Gogh to create this version of the painting less than a year prior to his death.

VAN GOGH'S LEGACY

THE RISE OF FAUVISM

Given that Van Gogh felt misunderstood throughout his life, it is perhaps unsurprising that his unusual style is particularly difficult to categorise within any specific artistic movement. He never founded a movement of his own, and the only label that can be attached to his work with any degree of accuracy is "Postimpressionist", which is not even a style or artistic movement *per se*, and instead simply denotes the period of time when he was active. Nevertheless, a short time after his death, Van Gogh's work became the main source of inspiration for two major modern art movements: Fauvism and Expressionism.

The leading figures of Fauvism were the French painters Henri Matisse (1869-1954), Georges Rouault (1871-1958), Albert Marquet (1875-1947), Maurice de Vlaminck (1876-1958), Kees van Dongen (1877-1968) and André Derain (1880-1954). In the same way that Van Gogh believed that the use of intense colour should express meaning in its own right, Fauvism was defined by its use of lurid, almost startling blocks of colour, which led the French art critic Louis Vauxcelles (1870-1943) to describe them as *"fauves"* (French for "wild beasts"), inadvertently coining the name of their movement.

After an exhibition of Van Gogh's work in Berheim in 1901, Vlaminck is reported to have exclaimed "I love Van Gogh better than my own father!" Whether or not this is true, the Dutch painter's influence is palpable in Vlaminck's painting *The Gardener* (1904), particular in terms of the use of colour. Similarly, the subject, the use of intense colour and the irregular brushstrokes used to evoke the sky and the field of wheat in his painting *The Farmer* (1905) are reminiscent of Van Gogh's *The Painter on the Road to Tarascon* (1888).

Furthermore, Matisse's *Self-Portrait in a Striped T-shirt* (1906) clearly draws inspiration from Van Gogh's *Portrait of Eugène Boch* (1888). While the subject is positioned in a classic three-quarter view, Matisse's use of colour to create the contours of his face is a clear homage to Van Gogh's work.

A NEW ARTISTIC LANGUAGE

Van Gogh's use of curved lines that echoed his inner emotional turmoil gave art a new purpose: to provide painters with an opportunity to express their own personality. The subject of the painting was no longer the artist's main concern; instead, they began to focus more on the style, which became a reflection of their own subconscious. This new way of understanding art eventually led to the rise of Expressionism, an artistic movement which emerged just before the outbreak of the First World War and which was led by Edvard Munch (Norwegian painter, 1863-1944), Emil Nolde (German-Danish painter, 1867-1956), Franz Marc (German painter, 1880-1916), Ernst Ludwig Kirchner (German painter, 1880-1938), Max Beckmann (German painter, 1884-1950), Oskar Kokoschka (Austrian painter, 1886-1980), Egon Schiele (Austrian painter, 1890-1918) and Otto Dix (German painter, 1891-1969). Kirchner's painting *Nollendorfplatz* (1912) employs a similar upward-facing angle, tilted perspective and distorted lines to Van Gogh's *The Church at Auvers* (1890), as well as featuring a similar diverging road in the foreground. This sense of imbalance gives the scene a quasi-supernatural or even phantasmagorical atmosphere, creating a landscape that lies at the intersection between dreams, nightmares and reality.

Van Gogh's work also had a significant effect on the avant-garde art of the early 20th century in terms of both theme and style. His use of skewed lines allowed him to express an almost animist vision of nature, which was echoed in later works depicting landscapes that seem to practically live and breathe, such as *Landscape at Céret* (c. 1920-1921) by the Russian artist Chaïm Soutine (1893-1943). In this painting, the range of colours and the exaggerated distortion of the trees are very reminiscent of Van Gogh's *The Olive Trees* (1889).

Although Van Gogh's life was marked by pain and solitude, few artists in history can be said to have matched his creativity or left behind such an inspiring legacy. Like the peasants he understood so well, Van Gogh was a sower, and the seeds he scattered eventually sprouted into a whole host of avant-garde art movements. Despite living as an outcast whose genius went unrecognised until after his death, Van Gogh's work defined the course of artistic progress in the 20th century.

SUMMARY

- Vincent van Gogh was born in 1853, when the Industrial Revolution was in full swing and the modern age was truly dawning. However, many of his paintings eschew the trappings of modernity, and instead portray an idealised vision of the rural world, paying tribute to the simplicity of peasant life and nature. Van Gogh was the son of a preacher and was an extremely empathetic individual, which led him to frequently depict the habits and worries of normal people in his work, generally in a realist or naturalist style inspired by the work of the painter Jean-François Millet.
- Another source of inspiration for Van Gogh was *ukiyo-e*, a Japanese print style featuring simple line-work, fluid brushstrokes, flat colours and a lack of proportion between the framing and subject of the painting.
- He was also inspired by the work of the Impressionists, particularly in terms of their use of colour, and their influence can be seen in many of his works.

- Although he dreamed of creating an artistic community of his own, Van Gogh's unusual art style and personality meant that this dream was never realised; furthermore, he was never truly part of a specific artistic movement. However, he had a tremendous influence on later styles of modern art, particularly Fauvism, which was heavily inspired by his abundant use of intense colours.
- By pouring his own emotions into his artwork, Van Gogh also provided artists with a new means of expression, which led to the rise of Expressionism. Indeed, many of Van Gogh's paintings can be said to reflect his own state of mind, including his famous *Sunflowers* series, which depicts both healthy, blooming flowers that represent his ideal self and wilting flowers that represent his decline.
- One of the most distinctive characteristics of Van Gogh's work is his use of distorted brushstrokes, which reflects his inner emotional turmoil.

We want to hear from you!
Leave a comment on your online library
and share your favourite books on social media!

FURTHER READING

BIBLIOGRAPHY

- (No date) Archived correspondence of Vincent van Gogh. [Online]. [Accessed 23 July 2018]. Available from: <http://vangoghletters.org/vg/>

- Artaud, A. (1990) *Van Gogh le Suicidé de la société*. Paris: Gallimard.

- Aurier, G.-A. (1890) Les Isolés : Vincent Van Gogh. *Mercure de France*. Paris.

- Barielle, J.-F. (1984) *Vie et Œuvre de Van Gogh*. Paris: ACR édition-Vilo.

- Bonnafoux, P. (1997) *Van Gogh, le soleil en face*. Paris: Gallimard.

- Burty, P. (1878) Exposition universelle de 1878. Le Japon ancien et moderne. *L'Art*. 4(15).

- Coquiot, G. (1924) *Des Peintres maudits : Cézanne, Daumier, Gauguin, Lautrec, Modigliani, Rouault, Seurat, Sisley, Utrillo, Van Gogh. Paris: Delpeuch éditeur.*

- *Duret, T. (1916) Vincent Van Gogh. Paris: Berheim-Jeune éditeur.*

- Eitner, L. (2002) *Nineteenth Century European Painting*. Boulder: Westview Press.

- (2014) Exhibition Catalogue for *Van Gogh/Artaud. The Man Suicided by Society*. Paris: Musée d'Orsay.

- Heinich, N. (1997) *The Glory of van Gogh: An Anthropology of Admiration*. Trans. Leduc Browne, P. Princeton: Princeton University Press.

- Naifeh, S. and White-Smith, G. (2013) *Van Gogh: The Life*. London: Profile Books.

- Restellini, M. (2012) Press release for the joint exhibitions *Van Gogh : rêves de Japon and Hiroshige : l'art du voyage. Paris:* Pinacothèque.

- Terrasse, C. (1947) *Van Gogh*. Paris: Floury.

- Uhde, W. (2015) *Van Gogh*. London: Phaidon.

- Uitert (Evert van), Tilleborgh (Louis van) et Heugten (Sjraar van), Van Gogh. Peintures/dessins, Milan, Arnoldo Mondadori Arte, De Luca Edizioni d'Arte/Paris, Albin Michel, 1990.

- (2014) Van Gogh/Artaud au musée d'Orsay. *Beaux-Arts Magazine*.

- Van Uitert, E., Van Tilleborgh, L. and Van Heugten, S. (1990) *Vincent Van Gogh: Drawings*. Milan: Arnoldo Mondadori Editore.

- (2014) Vincent van Gogh Biography. *Biography. com*. [Online]. [Accessed 23 July 2018]. Available from: <https://www.biography.com/people/vincent-van-gogh-9515695>

ADDITIONAL SOURCES

- *Loving Vincent.* (2017) [Film]. Dorota Kobiela and Hugh Welchman. Dir. Poland/UK/USA: BreakThru Productions and Trademark Films.

- *Vincent.* (1987) [Film]. Paul Cox. Dir. Australia/Belgium: Daska Films, Kultureel Centrum Vooruit and Illumination Films.

ICONOGRAPHIC SOURCES

- *The Potato Eaters*, 1885, oil on canvas, 82 x 114 cm, Amsterdam, Van Gogh Museum. Royalty-free reproduction picture.

- *The Sower*, 1888, oil on canvas, 64 x 84.5 cm, Otterlo, Rijksmuseum Kröller-Müller. Royalty-free reproduction picture.

- *The Sunflowers*, 1888, oil on canvas, 92.1 x 73 cm, London, National Gallery. Royalty-free reproduction picture.

- *The Starry Night*, 1889, oil on canvas, 73.3 x 92.1 cm, New York, Museum of Modern Art. Royalty-free reproduction picture.

- *Bedroom in Arles*, 1889, oil on canvas, 57.3 x 73.5 cm, Paris, Musée d'Orsay. Royalty-free reproduction picture.

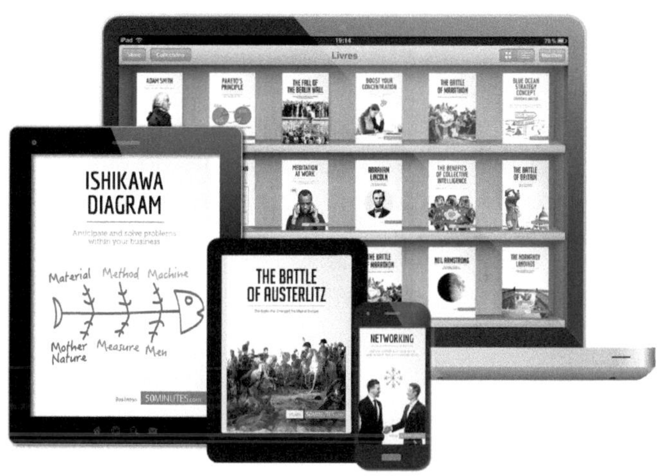

50MINUTES.com
History
Business
Coaching
Book Review
Health & Wellbeing
ISHIKAWA DIAGRAM
THE BATTLE OF AUSTERLITZ
NETWORKING
IMPROVE YOUR GENERAL KNOWLEDGE
IN A BLINK OF AN EYE !
www.50minutes.com